CRACKS IN THE CURIA

CRACKS IN THE CURIA

or,

Brother Choleric Rides Again

By
BROTHER CHOLERIC

SHEED AND WARD ·
LONDON AND NEW YORK

FIRST PUBLISHED 1972
SHEED & WARD LTD, 33 MAIDEN LANE,
LONDON WC2E 7LA

and

SHEED & WARD INC, 64 UNIVERSITY PLACE,
NEW YORK, N.Y. 10003

ISBN 0 8362 0490 5 . (U.S. edition)
0 7220 7211 2 . (U.K. edition)
Library of Congress Catalog No. 72–564

Made and printed in Great Britain by
William Clowes & Sons, Limited, London, Beccles and Colchester

For
Barbara Channer

who will now be able to add
to her psychological knowledge the
dementia cholerici

INTRODUCTORY NOTE

Brother Choleric began his *Cracks in the Cloister* drawings in 1955. By the end of 1962 and his fourth book he had said his say on the pre-conciliar Church, its nuns especially. Mother Superiors were picketing his monastery. So he started a rumour that he was dead, wrote his own obituary, and settled down to a life of indignant meditation. Somehow the news that the Second Vatican Council had changed things a bit drew him from his cell. *Cracks in the Curia* is his report on the changes.

Part I
PLUS C'EST LA MÊME CHOSE?

"While the Church has certainly relaxed many of its rules I'm afraid I can't accept both of you together into the novitiate."

"Please, Father, this is my first confession. Without regard to the encyclicals or the Declaration on Christian Education I have on a number of occasions assented to modernistic tendencies."

"I'd like to see them trying to frisk me for weapons at the border."

"Of course once they made angels redundant it could only be a matter of time before they classified us as wish fulfilments."

"Yes, Sister, here we have Masses in any language you care to choose—except of course the one the Church chose to use for upwards of eighteen hundred years."

IN SPITE OF ECUMENISM AND THE CHANGES
IT IS DOUBTFUL IF WE SHALL EVER HEAR:

*1. "Reverend Mr Paisley? This is the parish
priest of Ballymacaroon...the boys and I are
askin' ye to have a bit of dinner with us
tonight...ah, grand, grand."*

*2. "But don't you think as a candidate at the
next papal conclave Hans Küng is too
conservative?"*

3. "How about tacking a bit on at the end of Mass—say the first fourteen verses of St John's gospel?"

4. "I call it pretty decent on the part of the liturgists, scripture scholars, speculative theologians to admit that all along they had been talking complete bosh."

"I wonder if you can tell me the meaning of 'collegiality?'"

"Let me introduce, Reverend Mother, a group of the Lord's Anointed—just ordained."

"As far as I can make out he's appealing for a silence-in."

"No charges so far. Brother is just helping with enquiries."

"How charmingly pre-Council . . . and doesn't it take one back?"

"Forgive me, Sir George, I have still got the whole of today's Office to say. I'll be back in five minutes."

"Oh, so that's Becket. I must say I couldn't make head or tail of his Waiting for Godot.*"*

"On the left for saying Mass in English before the Decree...on the right for saying Mass in Latin after the Decree."

"We have to keep pretty fit these days—with all the hopping up and down at the Missa Normativa.*"*

"You don't suppose it could be the Berrigans?"

"I will say this about the new Easter Rite—that it does make for greater flexibility."

Part III
ET ANGELI ET ANGLI

"I see many clever gentlemen talking about you.
I fear the outlook for you gentlemen is not good.
Oh dearie me, not at all *good."*

"*You know that bit about how many angels can fit on the top of a pin? Well I've never seen why they should want to.*"

"The current style in the world being what it is, don't you think our brother of Hippiopolis would be well advised to modify his appearance?"

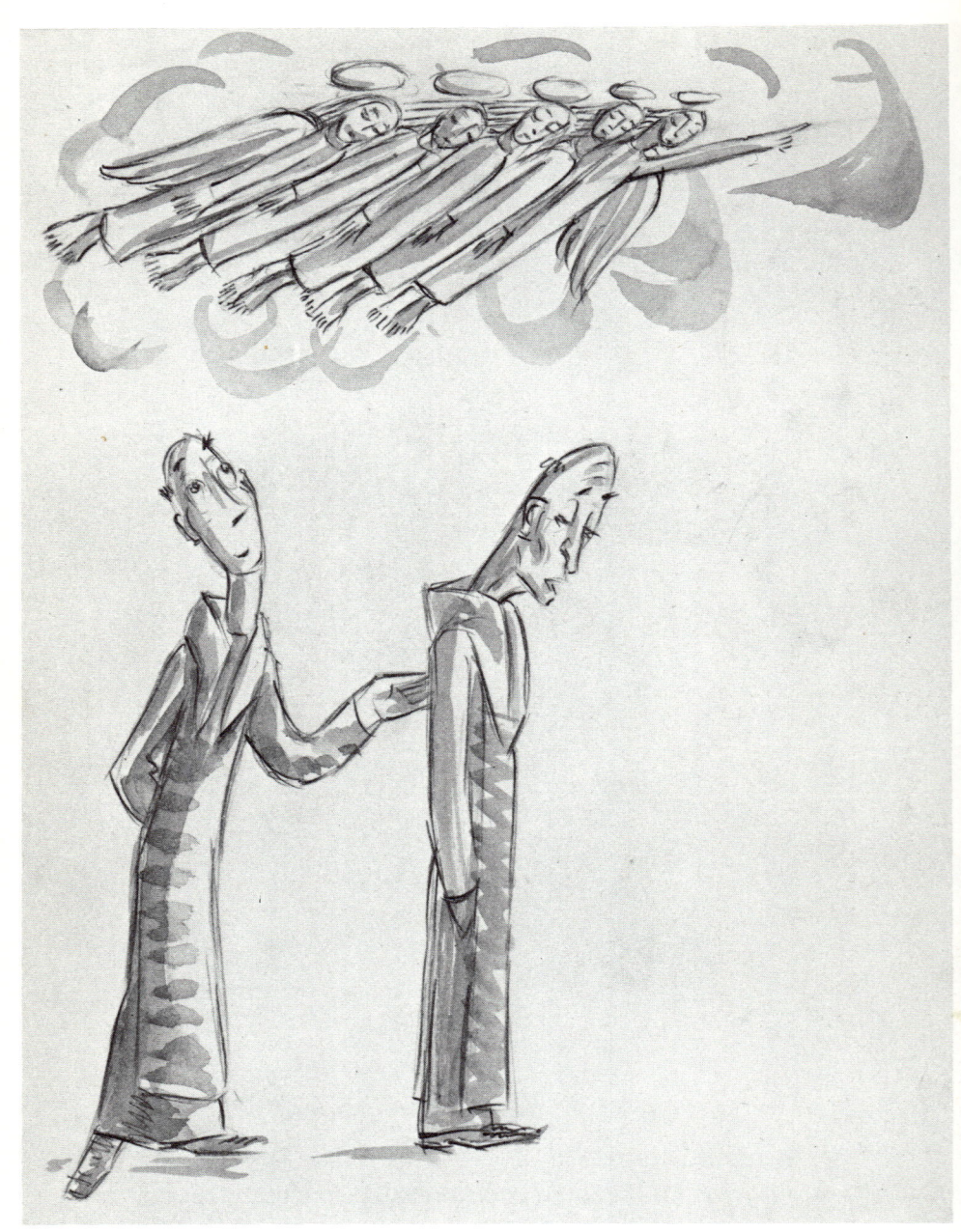

"Yes, we get a lot of them at this time of the year . . . migrating you know."

"Clerical collars, Father? We don't stock them any more. There's no demand today—except of course from among the clergy of other denominations."

"Funny hats these chaps wear."

"I say, I wonder if I could be on my front for this...I moult so easily."

"Well, so much for the jolly old dialogue."

"What are all those clever theologians saying down there? They're saying we don't exist. That's what they're saying."

"Cheer up, Sister—theologians tell us that when we get our celestial bodies we won't feel the cold."

Part IV
NEWSPEAK IN THE NUNNERY

"I ask myself—where will it all end?"

*"It's in excellent condition, and works like this.
I thought it would be nice for Reverend
Mother's feast."*

*"When you see a vision, Sister, is it a repeat or
does it come to you live?"*

"But my dear darling Reverend Mother, you realise don't you that this wayout poetry which you object to so much goes slap back to St John of the Cross."

"Narcotics swoop imminent—pass it on."

"Sister, how would it look like this for a change?"

"Just because I do not claim to be infallible, Monsignor, there is no reason to believe that I am not."

*"I don't care what your bally computer says—
I'm not resigning."*

"No, Father, we're not late. They're just limbering up."

Part V
GENTLY FLOWS THE TIBER

*"I am a clerical gentleman clad all in white...
I am addressing many clerical gentlemen clad
all in red...the clerical gentlemen in red do not
like what I am saying...they do not like it one
little bit."*

"Up Guards and at 'em."

"If I had retired at seventy-five, where would I be today I'd like to know? I would be on the shelf, that's where I'd be."

"Guy here says he was denied the right to speak at the Council of Trent and doesn't want it to happen again. Do we take this up?"

"Naughty naughty Küng darling...down, I say, down."

"I haven't seen one of those for years. Easy to see whose side he's on."

"Only way to beat the Roman traffic jams."

"Well, the Church in Holland doesn't seem to be doing much of that finger in the dyke stuff today."

"The views of a certain Eminence who shall be nameless could do us much harm. But fortunately he will not be able to give them in Latin."

"When Stalin asked how many divisions the Vatican had got, you know I sometimes wonder whether . . ."

"No, not Wyatt Earp—just Choleric the Kid."

"Take note, brother, of our silent minority."

"Me—*square?*"

"I have that public image to think about."

"In Cubam altus-Joannes sum."

"Forgive me; I thought it was name *tapes you objected to."*

"Careful, careful. This part of the city is chock full of undercover agents."

*"I would remind you, Brother, that there's
nothing new about Women's Liberation."*

"Have you noticed how different he is since he was nominated Monk of the Year?"